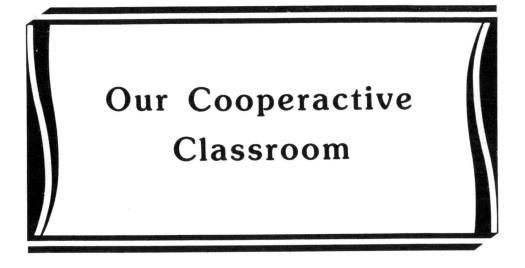

Our Cooperactive Classroom

David W. Johnson

Roger T. Johnson

Judy K. Bartlett

Linda M. Johnson

Interaction Book Company

7208 Cornelia Drive

Edina, Minnesota 55435

(612) 831-9500

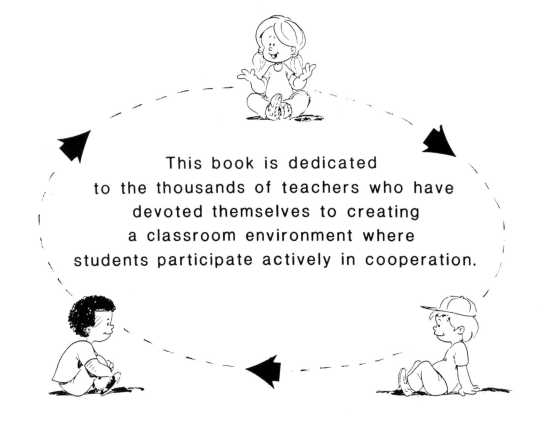

This book is dedicated
to the thousands of teachers who have
devoted themselves to creating
a classroom environment where
students participate actively in cooperation.

ISBN: 0-939603-05-5

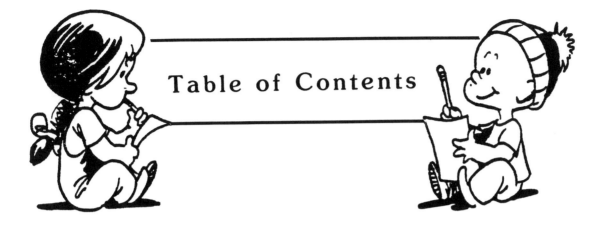

Table of Contents

Preface

Cooperative learning is an old idea. Shifting the emphasis from learning alone to caring about whether classmates are learning is a relatively simple idea. Yet it takes considerable skill by students and a reorientation as to how they should behave within learning situations. Students have to learn how to cooperate skillfully.

This book is to help students be better cooperators. Many critics of education point to the loss of cooperation within the family, community, and society. Students are not taught to understand their interdependence with others, to feel responsibility for meeting their obligations to others as well as helping and assisting others fulfill their obligations, to feel responsibility for the well-being of others as well as themselves, and to reach out to lonely and isolated peers.

The activities in this book are designed to assist students to develop a better understanding of and appreciation for cooperative learning by developing a personal understanding of cooperation and competition, being aware of what one and others can contribute to a cooperative effort, increasing their understanding of what cooperation is, knowing how to form and learn about their group, increasing their understanding of how to be a skilled and contributing group member, having them practice solving group problems, and pointing them to cooperate as an entire class and school.

As the activities of this book are completed, students will have repeated opportunities to work cooperatively with each other. This need to be a skillful cooperator is vital for today's youth as they begin training for leadership in a highly interdependent society and world. Herein lies the challenge of the present and the hope for a better future.

Our cooperative well of ideas constantly needs replenishing. We find that our best source for inspiration is you, the classroom teacher, and we welcome any suggestions for activities that you would share with us. If we select your contribution to include in our next publication, we will acknowledge you on the activity page and provide you with a formatted copy of the activity and a book. Send your ideas to Judy Bartlett, Cooperative Learning Center, 202 Pattee Hall, University of Minnesota, Minneapolis, Minnesota 55455

We wish to thank Thomas Grummett for most of the drawings in this book.

SECTION 1

COOPERATION

COMPETITION

On this page build a collage of people working or playing **Cooperatively.** Cut out pictures of cooperative activities and paste them in the frame below.

If you don't have magazines or newspapers, draw a picture in the frame of a cooperative activity.

COOPERATION

Now see how many words you can think of that remind you of **Cooperation.** Write them on the lines below. (We've put in a few to get you started.)

we   sharing   group

In this frame we've given you space to build a collage of pictures you've found to show **Competition.** Just cut them out and past them in the frame.

If you'd rather, you can draw a picture of a competition.

COMPETITION

On the lines below, write words or phrases that you think are **Competitive** words. (We've included a few examples.)

loser   beat   against

_____   _____

_____   _____

_____   _____

_____   _____

_____   _____

Cooperation and Competition

There are a list of sentences below. If you think the sentence describes something that sounds or looks **cooperative,** draw a line from it to the **cooperation** picture. If you think it describes something **competitive,** draw a line from the sentence to the **competitive** picture.

> We'll have fun doing this together!

> Let's see if we can put our heads together and figure out the answer!

> O.K., Paul, run your fastest! We have to beat the other team!

> Four people, sitting in a circle, listening to one member reading a page in a workbook.

> I think I can get the best grade in the class on this paper!

Write a sentence that describes something cooperative.

_____

_____

Write a sentence that describes something competitive.

_____

Working Together

Listed below are three reasons why you will find that cooperation helps you, both in and out of school. You will:

1. Learn more and remember it longer.

2. Be able to "stand in friends' shoes" and look at things the way they do.

3. Make more friends and get to know others better.

Now it's your turn. What reasons can you think of to work with others to get things done? Please make a list below.

_____

_____

_____

_____

_____

5

Cooperation Is Where You Find It

Listed below are words which go with COOPERATION.
See if you can find each word and circle it. The
words can either go down or across. Discuss the
meaning of each word with your group.

together
sharing
we
encouraging
cooperate
caring
group
support
others
social skills

```
Q C A K F O T H E R S K
A O R H W E A J Q A R E
S O C I A L S K I L L S
M P E M Z P O G D I O H
W E L P S U P P O R T A
G R O U P C H L A C H R
O A S T X E A F L A P I
F T O G E T H E R R O N
R E N C O U R A G I N G
S O L I D M E V E N S L
H R T O N G E O N G E N
```

6

⋗◆⋖ Times Together and Alone ◆⋗⋖

Some activities are better if you do them alone, but most
are better if more than one does them. Look at the activities
below, and see how many persons you think would do each thing
best. Write that number in the box beside the activity.

Working on
the Computer

Reading a
Book

Coloring
Easter Eggs

Going
Camping

Building a
Snowman

Washing
Your Dog

Swinging

Playing a Song
in an Orchestra

Cooking a Meal

7

Cooperation in Fall

In October every year, as the skies turn a special bright blue and Jack Frost puts a nip in the air, we look forward to raking the leaves in the yard. Leaf raking is an activity which is much better done by a group. On the lines below, tell why you think this is true.

8

" COOPERATIVE QUOTES "

On the next two pages you will find sentences about cooperation. It will be your job to decide how the parts of the sentence fit together to make a whole cooperative idea.

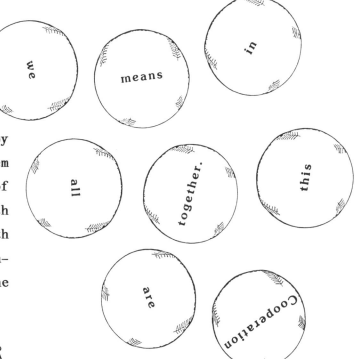

Hit a home run for cooperation by coloring the baseballs, cutting them out, and pasting them on a sheet of construction paper in an order which makes sense. (HINT: A word with a capital letter will start a sentence. Watch for the period at the end.)

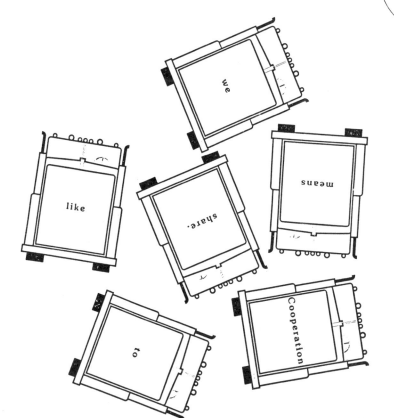

Now it's time to build a cooperative convoy. Color the trucks, cut them out and then paste them in order on a sheet of construction paper.

9

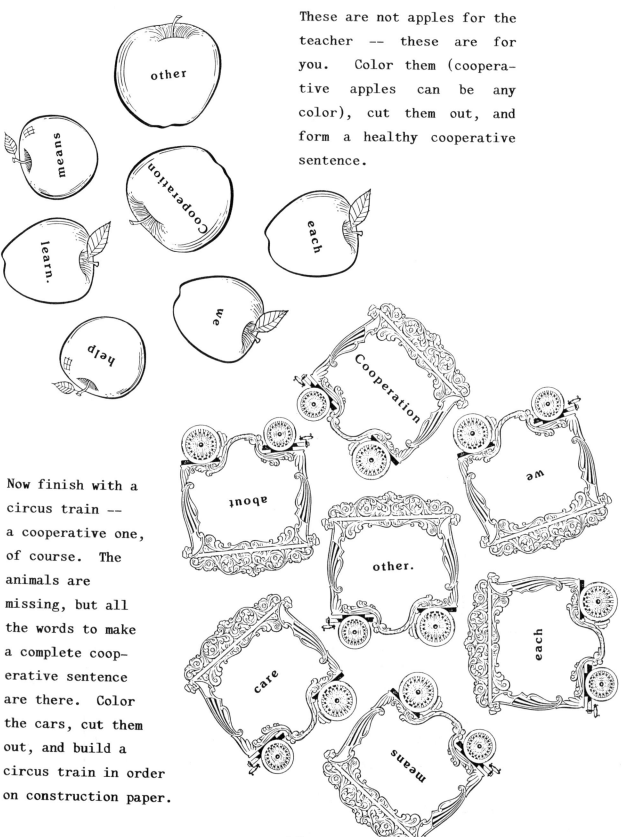

These are not apples for the teacher -- these are for you. Color them (cooperative apples can be any color), cut them out, and form a healthy cooperative sentence.

Now finish with a circus train -- a cooperative one, of course. The animals are missing, but all the words to make a complete cooperative sentence are there. Color the cars, cut them out, and build a circus train in order on construction paper.

SECTION 2

Knowing Myself

Knowing Others

KNOWING MYSELF

Hi!
I like you!

Learning to cooperate with others starts by getting to know yourself better. When you look in the mirror, you can see how you look to others. There are other things that make you special, though, that don't show when you look in the mirror. List five of the "hidden" ways you think you're special on the lines below.

_____

_____

_____

_____

_____

What one thing do you like most about yourself?

_____

_____

12

Read All About Me!

Pretend that you've bought an ad in a newspaper. In this ad you are going to tell people what would make you a good group member and why they would be glad if you were part of their group.

_____

_____

_____

_____

_____

Recognizing My Worth

I take good care
of plants . . . I
can help with
bulletin boards . . .

Think about the unique gifts and talents you
bring to your class. List them below.

Cut out the scroll and paste it on a sheet of
construction paper. Make a display of all
the scrolls in the class.

I, _____, bring these
special gifts and talents to my school
community:

_____

_____

_____

_____

_____

In Touch With Myself

In the top box below, tell how you think you show you are a cooperative person.

In the lower box, list things you do that may be uncooperative.

Name one thing you could do to make yourself a more cooperative person.

_____

_____

Sharing Myself

Bring into school a shoebox or another box about that size.

1. Put into the box at least three objects that are special to you. If the object you're thinking of is too large for the box, or if it is valuable and you don't want to bring it to school, draw or cut out a picture of that item.

2. Now decorate the outside of the box. Cut out words and pictures of:
   - Qualities that you have
   - Things you value
   - People whom you love
   Paste these words and pictures on the outside of your box.

3. Get into your group.

4. Pass the Sharing Boxes around the group. Take your time and silently examine each box carefully. Be sure and look both at the things inside the boxes and at the way the outsides are decorated.

5. Return each Sharing Box to its owner.

6. Take turns going around the group and share one thing you found very interesting about another person's box.

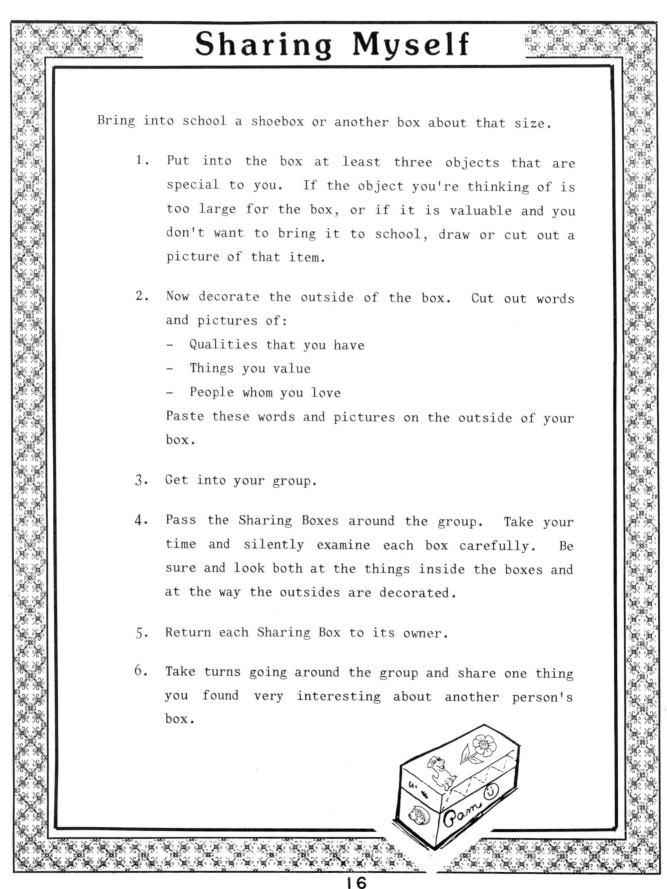

How Do Others See Me?

Sometimes other people see special things in us that we don't notice about ourselves. Below are four slips waiting to be filled out. Take each slip to the person shown on it and ask them to write something they really like about you on it. Bring the slip back to school, cut it out and put it in your Sharing Box.

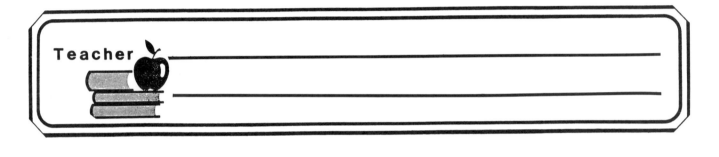

Teacher _____

_____

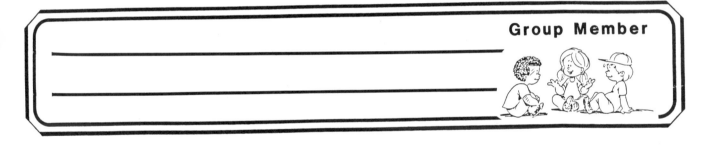

Group Member

_____

_____

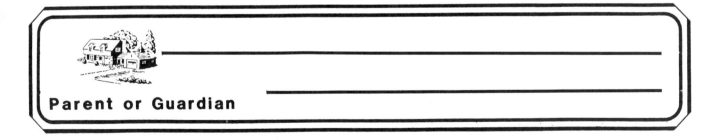

_____

_____

Parent or Guardian

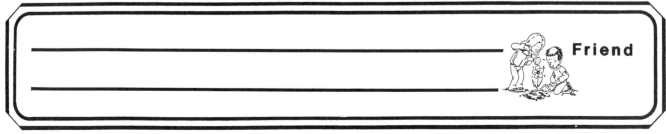

_____ **Friend**

_____

Sharing
Talents

Think about the unique
talents of your class-
mates.
Write the names of the
students with whom you
would like to accomplish
the following.

Building a clubhouse   _____

Planning a party   _____

Playing baseball   _____

Doing a science project   _____

Cleaning the yard   _____

Singing a song   _____

Baking a birthday cake   _____

Sharing a secret   _____

Telling a joke   _____

Going to the library   _____

Cheering up a sick friend   _____

**When you build your talent list by filling in the blanks,
see how many _different_ names you can use.**

Talent Hunt Jigsaw

Each student in the class
has something unique and
special to contribute.
Show how these talents fit
together to make each group
and then the class as a whole.

Materials Needed:

tag or poster board

scissors

magic markers

old magazines

white glue

cardboard

Procedure:

1. Cut a large piece of poster board or tagboard into enough
   pieces for each classmate and the teacher to have one.

2. On the puzzle piece have each person write one special gift
   he/she brings to the class. An option is to find a picture
   illustrating that quality and pasting it on the piece. Have
   each person sign his/her puzzle piece.

3. Have each person tell about his/her special talent.

4. Each group should fit its pieces together to form its section.

5. The groups should arrange their sections together to make the
   room puzzle.

6. Glue the completed puzzle to a piece of cardboard.

7. Hang the puzzle in a special place of honor within the classroom
   or school.

Linking the Class

Each group member should write his or her name on one of the links of the chain. Then he or she should paste on or draw a picture of something they treasure. After that step is complete, the group should staple or paste these links together. Next the group should design and color two group links which should be added at either end of the group chain. After each group has finished its link, a class chain can be built and hung from the ceiling or framing a bulletin board posted with cooperative sheets and activities.

SECTION 3

Experiencing Cooperation

PEOPLE POWER

This activity requires working together as a group.

Materials Needed:

paper cup

paper bag

table

Procedure:

Ask your classmates to kneel evenly around the table. Place the paper cup at one end of the table and the paper bag at the other end. At a given signal, join together in blowing the cup to the opposite end of the table. Work together until the cup drops into the bag. Do not touch the cup with your body. Repeat the procedure, seeing how much faster you can get each time.

Tell about your experiences with this activity in the space below:

_____

_____

_____

_____

Volleying Together

This activity changes the competitive game of volleyball to a cooperative group game.

Materials Needed:

2 blankets
1 volleyball (or similar ball)
volleyball net

Procedure:

Form two groups of eight to ten people. Members of each group should place themselves evenly around the outside of the blanket on either side of the volleyball net. Place the volleyball in the center of one blanket. At a given signal, snap the blanket and send the ball over the net, to be caught in the blanket of the opposite team. Pass the ball as quickly and as well aimed as possible.

Follow-Up:

Describe your feelings of participation in this cooperative activity:

_____

_____

_____

_____

_____

_____

23

Mirror Images

In order to be a cooperative member of your class,
you need to be aware of those around you.
The following activity is designed to make you notice
others around you.

Procedure:

Form in a circle of 12 to 15 students. Have one student stand in the center of the circle. The center student begins to move so that the other students can do the exact motions. Movements should be slow and simple. Take turns leading the group in mirroring the movements of others. (Note: This activity can also be done with two people taking turns in leading each other through mirroring movements.)

Follow-Up:

Tell about your mirroring movements in the space given below. Describe your feelings of cooperation while you were part of this activity.

_____

_____

_____

_____

_____

_____

Shoe Scramble

Form a circle with your classmates. Each person
in the circle must take off one shoe and place it
in the middle. When this has been done,
everyone must join hands. Then, without letting
go of the hands, each person must pick one shoe
other than their own, find the owner of the shoe,
and return it to him or her.

REMEMBER: Hands must be held at all times.
It will soon be very clear why this needs
to be a cooperative activity!

25

BIG TURTLE

Ask your teacher to divide the class
into four large groups. Each group
is going to build its own turtle shell,
using a large piece of cardboard or two pieces
of tagboard, taped together.
Your group is going to work cooperatively to design
and color the shell. Use your imagination.
Cooperative shells can be very colorful!

After you have built the shell, your group should gather under it.

With everyone on their hands and knees, place the shell over

the whole group. You are now a Big Turtle!

You have to think like one big turtle,

instead of separate human beings. Pretend you are heading

for your favorite lake on a hot, sunny day.

The more cooperation there is under the shell, the faster

you will get to the cool lake. Decide which direction

the lake is in and see if you can get there without losing your shell.

Take turns in positions under the shell.

26

Select a classmate to pair up with for this activity.
You will need a soft ball -- a Nerf ball
or a similar one.
You are going to pass the ball gently back and forth
between you.
As each of you tosses the ball, you are going to add
a letter to a word you are spelling, making it a combination
Cooperative Ball Toss and Cooperative Spell Down!

To practice this activity, start with something easy, like the letters in the alphabet. As you get quicker at the A-B-C toss, move up to a Category Toss. Take turns choosing a category. Then all the spelled words will fall into the chosen category. (For instance, if the category is THINGS TO EAT, you would start with a word like banana. When the two of you have spelled that word, the person who added the final letter selects the next word -- cake.

Spelling Toss will also be a good way to practice your spelling word list for the week. Go through the list, spelling each word as you toss the ball back and forth. The person not saying the letter must check to make sure his or her partner gave the right letter.

A few important rules to remember while using your Spelling Ball:
1. Use quiet voices. Remember that others are working on their words at the same time.
2. The ball must be tossed gently. This is a cooperative activity.

27

Project Snowman

On the next page you will find a friendly, smiling snowman. In order to keep him happy, there are a few important things your group of three will have to do.

1. Color the snowman in your group, taking turns with the crayons.

2. Finish dressing the snowman by giving him his two missing buttons.

The buttons are going to be pinned on the snowman in a special, cooperative way. Ask your teacher to put the colored snowman on the wall in a spot that's clear and somewhere that you can reach. Two of the group members are going to be the Direction Givers and the third is going to be the Dresser. The Dresser will be blindfolded and it is this person's job to listen carefully to the directions given by the other two members of the group. They will guide the Dresser to the snowman, using clear directions so that he or she will be able to pin on the buttons quickly. Practice with words like: <u>higher</u>, <u>lower</u>, <u>right</u>, <u>left</u>, and **so** on.

Take turns as Dresser and Direction Giver in your group and see if you can get better and better at giving and taking the directions.

28

29

COOPERATIVE CATEGORIZING

You'll need a partner for this activity. You will take turns choosing categories from which to construct your word lists. Possible categories include: foods, T.V. shows, games, furniture, clothes, etc.

The person choosing the first category names one thing that fits into the category and writes it on his or her list. The other person must then think of something in that same category which begins with the last letter in the other person's word. (For example, if the category chosen was FOOD, the first person might start with pear. Then other person might answer with rice.) The second person writes the word on his or her list. The round ends when neither of the partners can think of a word beginning with the ending letter of the word before.

You may have played a version of this game in your car. Remember that this is cooperative. You are not trying to get the other person out. You are trying to build two lists as long as possible. So it's your job to think of words which help the other person. Avoid any words which end in letters like x or even e because there are not many words which begin with those letters. Do not use plurals either because you will soon run out of words in the category beginning with the letter s.

The last part of this activity is to trade lists and check each other's spelling. Tell the other person if you find a word which you think is misspelled. If you cannot come to agreement on the spelling, check it in the dictionary.

WINNERS!

Your group of six has just won an all-expense-paid vacation for one week to the vacation spot of your choosing. Of course, it counts as a field trip, so that week you will have no school. Now comes the hard part -- where will your group choose to go??

In order to make that choice, break down into pairs. Each pair will think up a list of four places that would be special to them to visit. The pairs will write down their choices and talk over reasons why they think their choices are wise ones. (A trip to someone's grandparents' house may be a fine choice, if that person can suggest things that all the group members would enjoy there.)

After each pair has made its selection of four places, the group meets again to choose a final vacation spot. The group must reach consensus in order to claim their prize.

MY GROUP CHOSE TO VISIT

_____

ONE REASON I WOULD LIKE TO VISIT THERE IS:

_____

_____

_____

31

⋆⟶❊ THE MEMORY TASK ❊⟵⋆

Join one other member of your group to form a pair. Your cooperative task will be a MEMORY TASK. You and your partner will help each other learn as many lines of the poem below as you can. See if you can think of ways to make this learning job easier for your partner.

NOTE: You may choose to learn another poem instead of this one. Choose one which is at least ten lines long.

One there was an elephant
Who tried to use the telephant
No, no... I mean an elephone
Who tried to use the telephone
Oh, dear, I am not certain, quite
If, even now, I've got it right.
Well, anyhow, he got his trunk
Entangled in the telefunk --
The more he tried to get it free
The louder buzzed the telefee.
I think I'd better drop the song
Of elefop and telefong.

FEEDBACK: By yourself, think over the following statement and put your answer on the lines. Then share it with your partner and listen carefully to his or her statement about your help.

Partner, it helped when you _____

_____

_____

Island Adventure

Ask your teacher to assign groups of four for this activity.

Your group has decided it would be fun to vacation together in Hawaii. You have all boarded the jet and are over the ocean, talking about all the things you are going to do when you land.

Fate steps in, however, and all your plans fly out the window. There is a sudden loss in air pressure in the plane, and the pilot tells you that you will need to put on your parachutes and leave the plane.

Your group is the first off the plane and so when you land, you are very close together and soon have found all the members of your group. Luckily, you have all landed safely, without injury, and even though you are not in Hawaii, it could have been much worse!

You have arrived on a small, deserted (besides your group) desert island. It might well be months before you are found. But you don't have much to worry about because there are coconuts, berries and fish to eat. There is a stream of fresh water running through the island and caves to live in. The weather is warm and sunny. Your needs for keeping alive are all available right there on the island.

THE MOST IMPORTANT CONSIDERATION NOW IS GETTING ALONG WITH EACH OTHER AND HELPING EACH OTHER.

(Cont. on next page)

ISLAND ADVENTURE

(continued)

Now your group needs to buckle down and come up with some good rules for life on your island. Your first task is to spend ten minutes thinking up a name for the island. Come to consensus on one which all of you will think of as home for a while. Then if time permits, your group can design a flag or banner with the name of the island. Color the banner and put it on the wall where the whole group can see it.

The most important part follows. Your group will take ten minutes and discuss all the rules for living you think will be important on the island. One of the group will write down these rules as you think of them.

Aften this ten minutes is up, the next ten minutes will be spent deciding which of the rules will be most important for the good of the whole group. Choose seven rules which you agree are most vital for your survival and for getting along well with each other. Put a star by these seven as you talk about them. After this ten minutes has passed, write your group's rules on a sheet of paper to share with the class.

34

SECTION 4

Forming
Groups

Forming Groups

Here are four students who are about to get into
(**form**) their group. What skills can you think of that
are very important to do this well? List one by each
of the group members.

✈ The Cooperative Classroom ✦

This illustration shows a classroom arranged well for group work. How a room is set up is important for good group learning. One of the things we can tell from this picture is that students are working in groups of three. Three is a very good number for working together. Do you notice any other things that show this is a good cooperative arrangement? List them on the lines below.

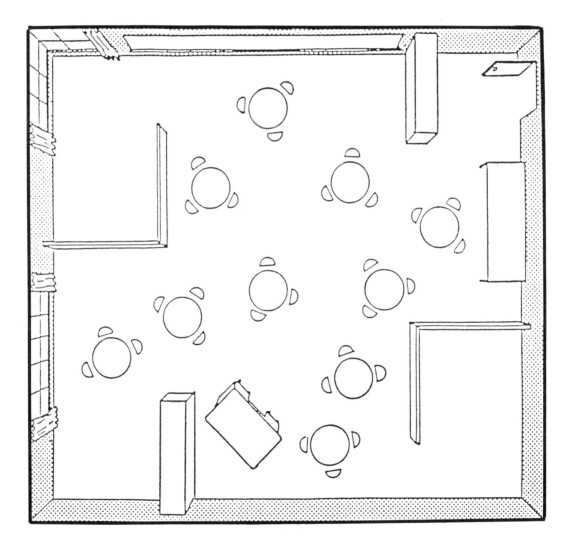

A Time for Cooperation

One of the most cheerful signs of winter is the smiling face of a friendly snowman. If you think back to the last time you built one in your yard, you will probably picture it as a group activity. Most likely more than one was involved in building it. There are many other winter activities which work best when several people are cooperating. On the lines below write as many of these activities as you can think of. Look at the pictures on the page to give you clues, but see if you can up with some other ideas also.

SECTION 5

Learning About

My Group

Building a Bridge
Among Group Members

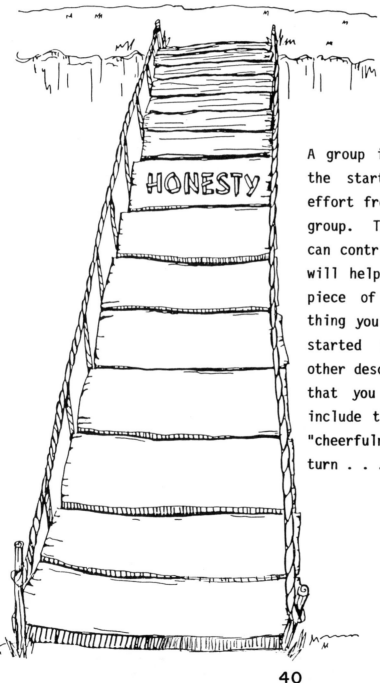

A group is not strong right from the start. It will take some effort from you to make it a good group. There are many things you can contribute to the group which will help this process. On each piece of the bridge, write one thing you think will help. We've started with honesty; you add other descriptive words or actions that you think of. (You might include things like "a smile" or "cheerfulness." Now it's your turn . . .

Complete the statements below by finding the member of your group who best fits into each category. Put that person's name on the appropriate line. You will be surprised how much you will learn about your group and how much they will learn about you!

1. A person in this group who has the same color eyes as mine is _____.

2. The person in this group whose last name starts with the letter closest to mine is _____.

3. A person in this group who was born in a different state is _____.

4. A person in this group who is taller than I am is _____.

5. A person in this group who has a pet is _____.

6. The person in this group who lives farthest from me is _____.

7. A person in this group who likes my three favorite TV programs is _____.

8. A person in this group who likes avocados is _____.

9. A person in this group who likes the same sports I do is _____.

10. A person in this group whose favorite subject is the same as mine is _____.

GROUP MOBILE

MATERIALS

- Circles from next page
- Group name tag strip
- Individual name tag strip
- Poster board or tagboard squares
- Scissors
- Glue
- Old magazines
- Crayons
- Paper punch
- Yarn or string

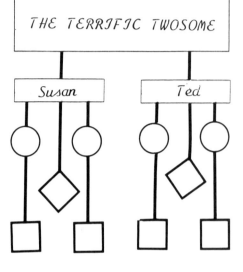

PROCEDURE

- Meet with your group and select a name that is chosen with group consensus.

- Together decorate the group name tag strip and write your selected name on the strip.

- Work individually to decorate the personal name tag strips.

- Glue the completed circles from the next page onto tagboard and cut out around the circles.

- On one of the square pieces of tagboard, cut out a picture which illustrates your favorite hobby.

- On another piece of tagboard, write the name of your favorite book and draw a picture showing what it is about.

- On another square, glue a picture of your favorite food.

- Punch three holes evenly along the bottom of your personal name tag strip and one hole at the top of each of the two circles and one of the squares. Tie them to the name strip with the yarn or string, with the square in the center. Take the remaining two squares and fasten them in the same way to the bottom of the two circles.

- Then take the group name and fasten the individual name tags to the bottom. Ask your teacher or custodian to hang the group mobiles somewhere in your classroom.

42

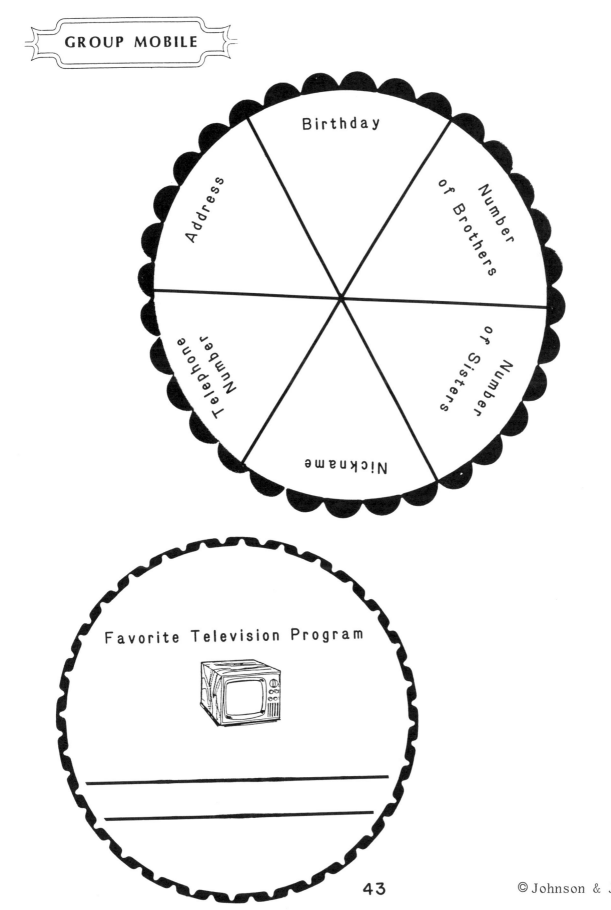

Birthday

Address

Number of Brothers

Telephone Number

Number of Sisters

Nickname

Favorite Television Program

SPRING FLING

When the weather begins to warm up in spring, there are a number of things you can find to do together. You see a picture of a group of boys and girls busy with one of these activities -- running a lemonade stand. There are several tasks involved in taking care of this project. Can you list some of the things that need to be done in order to make this stand a success? Can you see why cooperation is important in this project?

SECTION 6

Being a Good Group Member

Being a
Good Group Member

Sometimes a boy or girl doesn't remember what it means to be a good group member. What are some things you could share with the boy in the picture that **YOU** do to help your group?

I _____ .

I _____ .

I _____ .

I _____ .

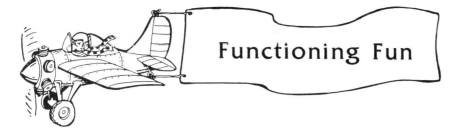

Functioning Fun

While your group is working on a task, there are many things to do that will make the group's work better. These are called **functioning** skills. You will find the definitions of some **functioning** skills on the left side of this page. See if you can fit the answers into the crossword puzzle. (If you need a little help thinking of the words, turn the page upside down and you will see a list of them.)

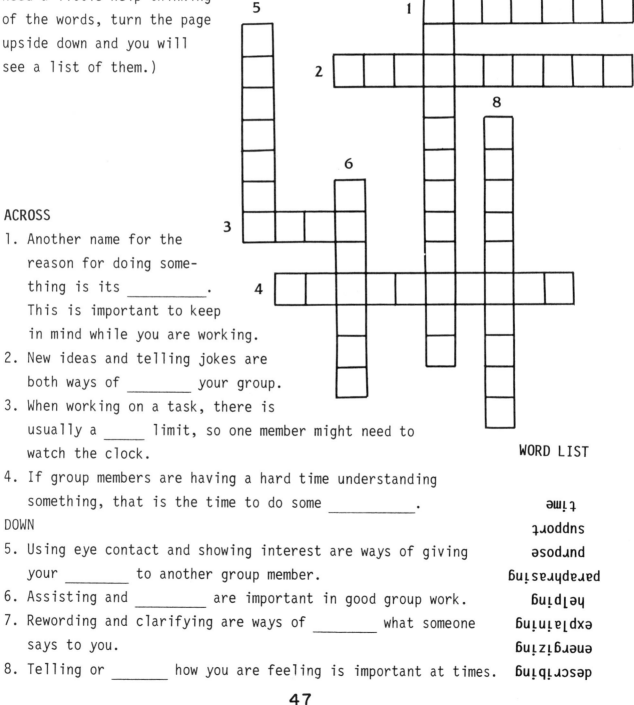

ACROSS

1. Another name for the reason for doing something is its _____. This is important to keep in mind while you are working.
2. New ideas and telling jokes are both ways of _____ your group.
3. When working on a task, there is usually a _____ limit, so one member might need to watch the clock.
4. If group members are having a hard time understanding something, that is the time to do some _____.

DOWN

5. Using eye contact and showing interest are ways of giving your _____ to another group member.
6. Assisting and _____ are important in good group work.
7. Rewording and clarifying are ways of _____ what someone says to you.
8. Telling or _____ how you are feeling is important at times.

WORD LIST

time
support
purpose
paraphrasing
helping
explaining
energizing
describing

Our Group Goal

One of the most important things to remember about working in cooperative groups is that we "sink or swim together."
A name for this is <u>positive interdependence</u> which means that we work together in a good way to make exciting things happen.

One way that we see positive interdependence in action is when we have a group goal. This is a task that all the members of our group have to work together on in order to complete it. It may be a math sheet with problems or a science experiment or reading a story in your book together. Each member of the group contributes ideas and works to finish the job.

This is an assignment for your group. Get together and choose a topic which you are all interested in. Now you are going to write eight sentences on that topic, with each group member taking a turn. You will be going around the circle twice. When one of the members is thinking of his or her sentence, the other members may suggest ideas. The only person who can write the sentence, though, is the one whose turn it is.

See what a good story you can build with the eight sentences. Think of the sentence which came before yours when it is your turn. Build on that idea in your sentence.

Your group goal is the completed story, with each group member contributing two sentences within the story and giving his or her ideas while others are working.

Share your story with the rest of your class and see how many different topics groups chose.

Group Reward

You will also experience <u>positive interdependence</u> when your teacher gives you a group reward for completing a task well. This reward may come in many ways. Your teacher may decide that your group deserves an extra 15 minutes on the playground. He or she may award you a group certificate to put on the wall above your group. What rewards do you think your group would like to get for a job well done?   List a few on the lines below.

_____

_____

_____

_____

_____

_____

_____

_____

GROUP TASK ROLES

Pretend that your group has just started a cooperative science project--
setting up a group aquarium. To give this project positive interdependence, your teacher has assigned certain roles. Below you will see the
roles for this project. On the lines next to each role, write a
sentence describing what you think the responsibilities of each group
member will be.

Fish Tender: _____

_____

_____

Aquarium Manager: _____

_____

_____

Marine Life Reader: _____

_____

_____

Project Checker:

_____

_____

_____

_____

Cooperative Skills Game

On the following four pages you will find a board game called: Cooperative Skills. Not only will you have fun playing the game, but, if you read all the boxes carefully as you pass by them, you will have a good start on learning the cooperative skills.

You will need to do a few things to get the game ready to play. First, choose a color for each of the skills areas. (For example, color all the Forming skills red, all the Funtioning skills yellow, all the Formulating skills green, and all the Fermenting skills blue.) After you have colored all the skills areas, paste the two sheets on one big piece of construction paper or tagboard. Make sure the page with START is on the left and the page with FINISH is on the right.

Your second job before the game begins is to cut out Skills Cards and mix them up carefully. Put them on a pile face down beside your game board.

You will need a partner to play the game. (Three or four can also play if there are enough people.) You will also need a marker to move for each player and a die to roll.

To start the game, each player rolls to see who has the highest number. That person starts, and the others follow in clockwise order around the table. The markers all begin on the START arrow. Play moves around the board. When a player lands on a space marked SC, he or she draws a SKILL CARD and follows the directions on it. Players should slide right over the SLIDE arrow, moving directly to the space marked FORMULATING. The first player or team to reach the finish arrow chooses another player to help to FINISH until everyone has passed over all the skills.

© Johnson & Johnson

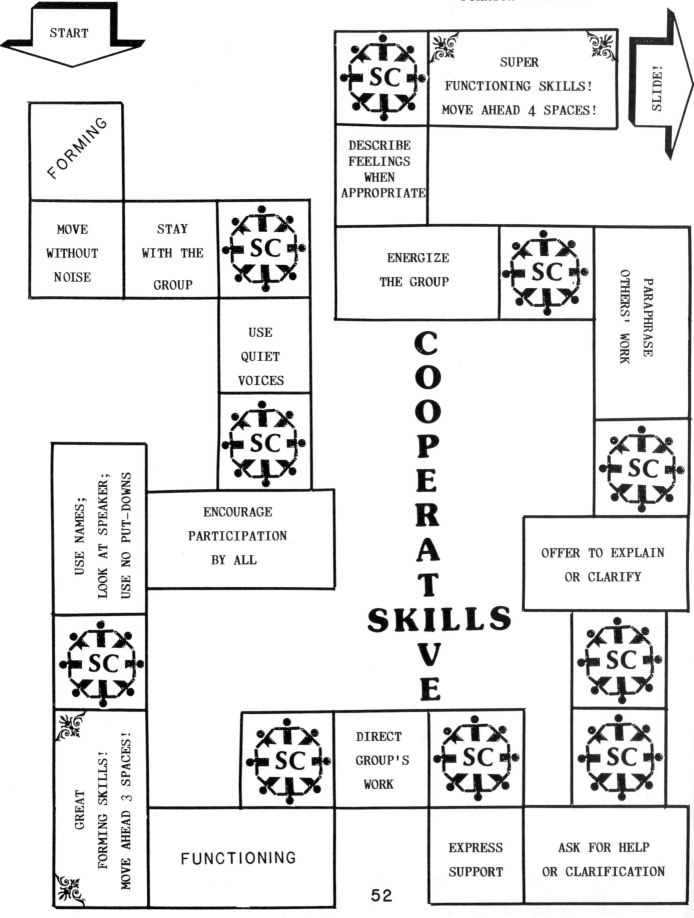

START

© Johnson & Johnson

FORMING

SUPER
FUNCTIONING SKILLS!
MOVE AHEAD 4 SPACES!

SLIDE!

MOVE
WITHOUT
NOISE

STAY
WITH THE
GROUP

SC

DESCRIBE
FEELINGS
WHEN
APPROPRIATE

USE
QUIET
VOICES

ENERGIZE
THE GROUP

SC

PARAPHRASE
OTHERS' WORK

SC

USE NAMES;
LOOK AT SPEAKER;
USE NO PUT-DOWNS

ENCOURAGE
PARTICIPATION
BY ALL

C
O
O
P
E
R
A
T
I
V
E

SKILLS

SC

OFFER TO EXPLAIN
OR CLARIFY

SC

GREAT
FORMING SKILLS!
MOVE AHEAD 3 SPACES!

SC

DIRECT
GROUP'S
WORK

SC

SC

FUNCTIONING

EXPRESS
SUPPORT

ASK FOR HELP
OR CLARIFICATION

52

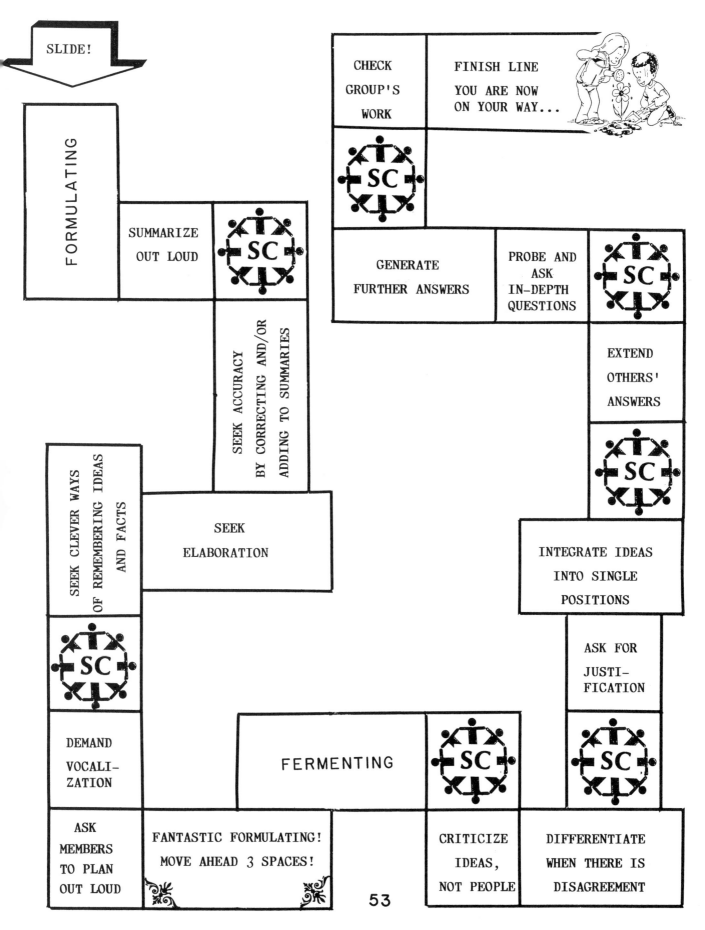

SLIDE!

FORMULATING

SUMMARIZE OUT LOUD

SC

SEEK ACCURACY BY CORRECTING AND/OR ADDING TO SUMMARIES

SEEK CLEVER WAYS OF REMEMBERING IDEAS AND FACTS

SEEK ELABORATION

SC

DEMAND VOCALIZATION

ASK MEMBERS TO PLAN OUT LOUD

FANTASTIC FORMULATING! MOVE AHEAD 3 SPACES!

FERMENTING

SC

CRITICIZE IDEAS, NOT PEOPLE

CHECK GROUP'S WORK

FINISH LINE YOU ARE NOW ON YOUR WAY...

SC

GENERATE FURTHER ANSWERS

PROBE AND ASK IN-DEPTH QUESTIONS

SC

EXTEND OTHERS' ANSWERS

SC

INTEGRATE IDEAS INTO SINGLE POSITIONS

ASK FOR JUSTI-FICATION

SC

DIFFERENTIATE WHEN THERE IS DISAGREEMENT

53

Skill Cards

You said to a group member:
"What are your ideas, David?"
Good work! Move ahead 2 spaces.

You reminded the group that
they only had fifteen minutes left
to work. Move ahead 1 space.

You asked each group member
if they had any other answers
to Question 7. Move ahead 1 space.

You told the group that
you were feeling sad when you couldn't
work the problem. Move ahead 2 spaces.

You remembered to use a quiet voice
when you were working in your group!
Good Forming Skills! Move ahead 1.

You remembered to keep your feet
under your own chair while working.
Move ahead 1 space.

You asked a group member to explain
why he felt his answer was correct.
Move ahead 2 spaces.

You said to another member of your
group: "You really worked hard on that
problem!" Move ahead 2 spaces.

You remembered to look
at the speaker when she was talking.
Move ahead 2 spaces.

You asked another member for help
when you weren't sure what the
question meant. Move ahead 1 space.

54

Skill Cards 🙪

You called another group member a name instead of criticizing his ideas. Move back 2 spaces.

You poked and bumped other group members while they were trying to work. Move back 2.

You wandered around the room instead of helping your group. Move back 1 space.

You moved your chair aside and worked alone on the problems. Move back 1 space.

You didn't contribute any ideas or answers to the group today. Move back 2 spaces.

You forgot to use other members' names when you were talking to them. Move back 1 space.

Your voice got very loud during group discussions. Move back 1 space.

You forgot to wait your turn and interrupted other members when they were talking. Move back 2 spaces.

You sat and pouted when the group chose a different answer from yours. Move back 2 spaces.

You asked the teacher for help instead of turning to the other members of your group. Move back 1.

55

For each of the social skills you learn and practice, there are special things that it looks like and things that it sounds like. Below you will find a **T-CHART**. This is a figure which will show us what the skill is. This time we are using the skill **ENCOURAGING**, a very important skill to use in your group. On the left side of the T-Chart, you will see room for a list of things Encouraging looks like. (We've given you one example.) On the right side of the T-Chart, you have space to write in what Encouraging should sound like. See if you can think of other **Looks Like** and **Sounds Like** for Encouraging and fill in the rest of this T-Chart.

ENCOURAGING

Looks Like	Sounds Like
Thumbs Up	"Good Idea!"

Another of the social skills to practice with your group is **CHECKING**. On the **T-Chart** below are listed two things you will see when checking is being done, and two other things you will hear. Fill in the rest of the chart with ideas you have for **Looks Like** and **Sounds Like**.

CHECKING

Looks Like	Sounds Like
Listening carefully to others' answers	"David, how did we get that answer for number two?"
Asking for explanations of answers	"Let's summarize what we've done on this page."

A social skill which is really fun
to practice is **PRAISING**. All of us like to **get**
praised, but you might be surprised to find how
much you'll also enjoy **doing** the praising!
You'll find an example for **Looks Like** and one
for **Sounds Like** in the T-Chart below.
Please see what great ideas you can come up with
to complete the chart.

PRAISING

Looks Like	Sounds Like
Patting on the back.	"Judy, you're very helpful."

Group Roles

When you are working in groups, you will often be given a role by your teacher. A **ROLE** is a special job that you will do in your group to help make it work better. Below are three roles you may be given by your teacher and names that we've chosen for each role. Can you think of another name that you would call the role?

Reader

This person reads the work out loud to the group, carefully and with expression, so that group members can understand and remember it.

Your Name: _____

Writer

This group member carefully records the best answers of the group on the worksheet or paper, gets other members to check and sign the paper, then turns it in to the teacher.

Your Name: _____

Materials Handler

This role is to get materials or equipment needed by the group, keep track of them and put them carefully away.

Your Name: _____

READER

Your teacher has chosen you to be the **READER** for your group. Think of what you will be doing as the Reader. List below two things that will be important for you to do as a Reader and two things you might say when you are doing the job of a Reader.

As a Reader, I will:

1. _____

_____

2. _____

_____

As a Reader, I might say:

1. _____

_____

2. _____

_____

Today you are going to be the **WRITER** for your group. What are you going to do as the Writer to help your group get their job done well? On the lines below, write two things the Writer does for the group and two things that you might be heard saying as a Writer for your group.

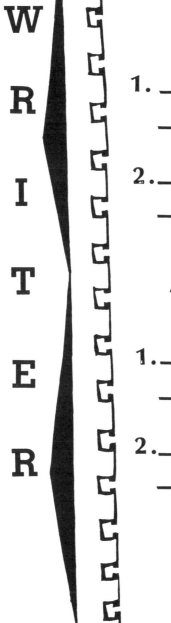

As a Writer, I will:

1. _____

   _____

2. _____

   _____

As a Writer, I might say:

1. _____

   _____

2. _____

   _____

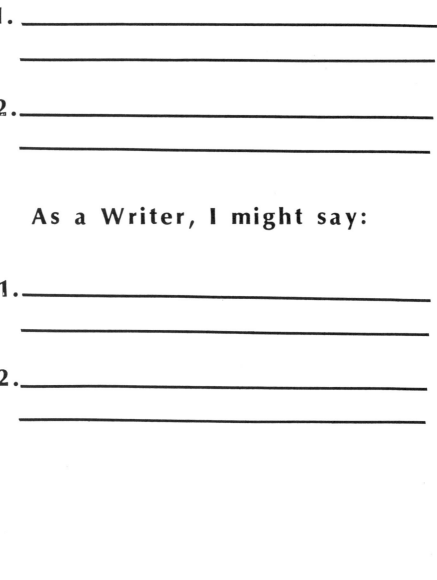

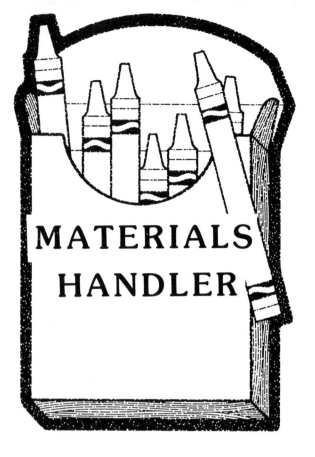

MATERIALS HANDLER

The next time you meet with your group, you are going to be the **MATERIALS HANDLER**. Think of your tasks in this role. What things are you going to do as a Materials Handler that will help your group? What things might your group members hear you say as a Materials Handler? List them below.

As a Materials Handler, I will:

1. _____

_____

2. _____

_____

As a Materials Handler, I might say:

1. _____

_____

2. _____

_____

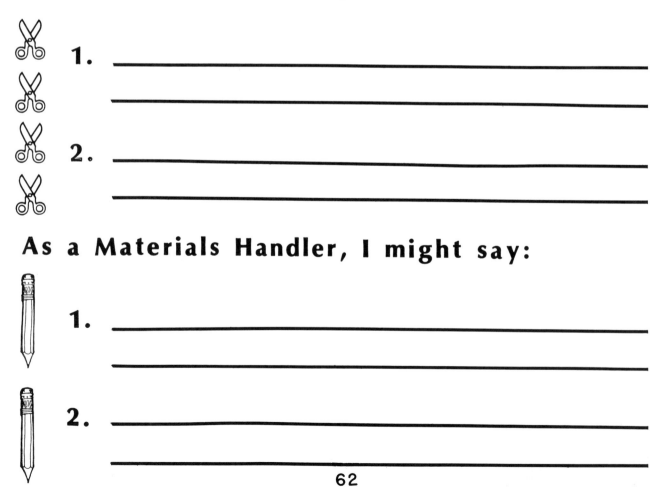

SECTION 7

Group
Skills

COOPERATIVE SKILLS RAINBOW

As a review of the cooperative skills, you're going to design a cooperative rainbow. Color in the different skills areas with rainbow colors, designs, or whatever your cooperative rainbow should look like.

Then spend a few minutes   thinking over the skills.
Write a few examples   from each area on the
lines next to it.

Fermenting

Formulating

Functioning

Forming

Successful
Cooperative
Groups

Forming _____

_____

Functioning _____

_____

Formulating _____

_____

Fermenting _____

_____

Communication Skills

It takes more than a large vocabulary to be a skilled communicator. Next to the sentences below rank yourself on each of the communication skills.

		Always	Often	Sometimes	Seldom	Never
1.	I have a warm smile.	5	4	3	2	1
2.	I have good eye contact.	5	4	3	2	1
3.	I make encouraging comments.	5	4	3	2	1
4.	I take time to listen.	5	4	3	2	1
5.	I make honest responses.	5	4	3	2	1
6.	I make cheerful responses.	5	4	3	2	1
7.	I thank people in my group for their help.	5	4	3	2	1

Write a sentence on the lines below telling the one thing you could work on to improve your communication.

_____

_____

_____

65

Listening

Listening is a very important part of communicating.
Listed below are characteristics of a good listener.

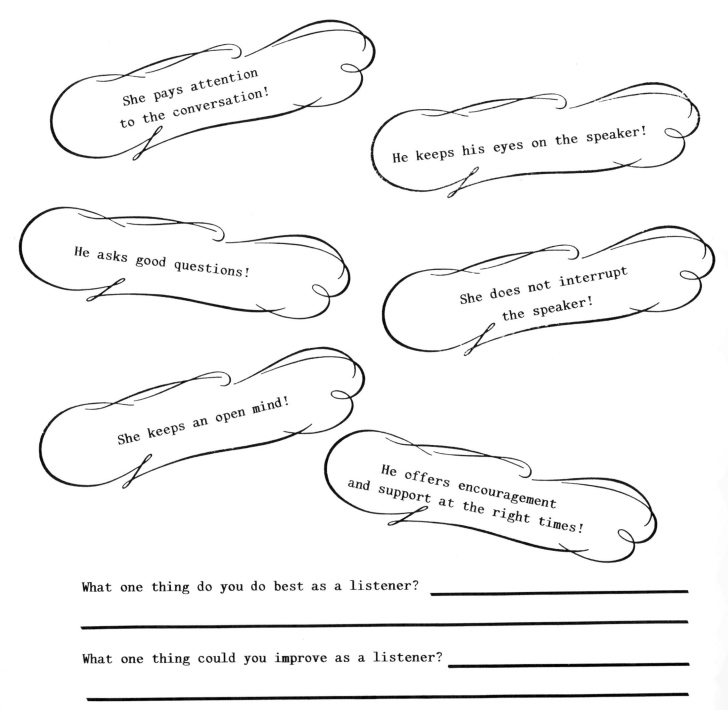

She pays attention to the conversation!

He keeps his eyes on the speaker!

He asks good questions!

She does not interrupt the speaker!

She keeps an open mind!

He offers encouragement and support at the right times!

What one thing do **you** do best as a listener? _____

_____

What one thing could you improve as a listener? _____

_____

Signal Sending

When you speak clearly and precisely, it is much easier for someone to understand you. Let's practice doing those two things with the following activity.

- Choose a partner.

- Select an object to be hidden in the room.

- One of your pair puts on a blindfold and is the detective.

- The other finds a good spot in which to hide the object and is the direction giver.

- It is the task of the direction giver to try and give as few directions as possible to assist the detective to find the object quickly.

- Take turns being the detective and the direction giver.

- See if you can improve your time in finding the object.

What did you learn from this activity?

_____

_____

_____

_____

_____

FEELINGS

List some words or phrases you might use if you felt the
following ways about something or someone.

love _____

_____

_____

anger _____

_____

_____

embarrassment _____

_____

_____

fear _____

_____

_____

thankfulness _____

_____

_____

Communicating Feelings

It is important to be able to express your feelings. How do you express yourself when you have the following feelings? Is there a way that you could express yourself better?

When I am angry, I sometimes

_____

_____

I might better express anger by

_____

_____

_____

When I am sad, I sometimes express myself by

_____

_____

I could express sadness better by

_____

_____

69

BODY TALK

BODY LANGUAGE is another way of communicating. As you react to different situations, your body takes on certain positions.

Picture yourself at times when you feel the emotions listed below. Describe how your body looks when you feel these ways.

Embarrassment _____

_____

Nervousness _____

_____

Excitement _____

_____

Boredom _____

_____

Now draw a line from each face below to the feeling it shows.

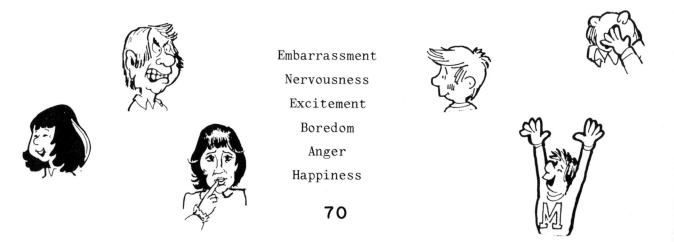

Embarrassment
Nervousness
Excitement
Boredom
Anger
Happiness

70

Leadership Skills

One of the really exciting things about working together in groups is that everyone can be a leader. All it takes is some practice and use of the leadership skills. See if you can list a few of those skills below. Think about them, use them, and become a group leader!

When I use leadership skills, I do the following:

_____

_____

_____

_____

When I use leadership skills, I might say:

_____

_____

_____

_____

_____

It is very important when working in cooperative groups that members are able to be <u>trusting</u> with each other. If you are trusting with the other members of your group, it means that you know you can share your feelings, thoughts, and ideas with them. You know that they won't laugh at you or make fun of the things you are telling them. See if you can think of some ways you can show you are trusting with others. List two of your ideas of what you do to show you are trusting and two things you might say when you are trusting.

When I trust someone, I show it by:

_____

_____

_____

_____

When I trust other group members, I might say:

_____

_____

_____

_____

TRUSTWORTHINESS

There is a perfect balance for <u>trust</u> within cooperative groups -- and that is <u>trustworthiness</u>. If your partner in a group shows that he trusts you, then you are trustworthy if you accept those thoughts, feelings, or ideas and listen to them with care. You show support for the other person and let him know that you would like to cooperate with him. See if you can think of ways to show trustworthiness.

I show trustworthiness by:

_____

_____

_____

_____

When I am being trustworthy, I might say:

_____

_____

_____

_____

CAR and DRIVER

You will choose a partner for this activity. One of you will be the <u>Car</u> and the other will be the <u>Driver</u>. The Driver stands directly behind the Car with her hands on the Car's shoulders. The Car will close his eyes and covers them with both hands. The Driver then directs the Car around the room, using hand signals and whispered instructions. The Driver must think about safety and consider others when giving the Car directions. After a few minutes, Car and Driver change places.

Write one sentence describing how the CAR is being TRUSTING. ———————————

———————————————————

———————————————————

———————————————————

———————————————————

Write one sentence describing how the DRIVER is being TRUSTWORTHY. ———————

———————————————————

———————————————————

———————————————————

———————————————————

⇝ Disagree With Ideas, Not People ≋

When you're working in your group, it's very important to remember to direct your disagreement toward the ideas which were discussed. Do not criticize the person making the suggestion. Picture how you feel when someone criticizes you. Practice this skill by completing the sentences below.

If I disagree with an idea expressed by another group member, I might say:

_____

_____

_____

_____

_____

_____

75

OBSERVATION SHEET

Group Members: _____

_____

Behaviors Observed:

Working Together: _____

Sharing Information: _____

Discussing Pros and Cons: _____

Listening and Explaining: _____

Using Quiet Voices: _____

Complimenting Good Behavior: _____

TOTAL TALLY MARKS: _____

Divide by 5: _____

TOTAL BEHAVIOR POINTS: _____

GROUP PROCESSING

What skills were you practicing?

_____

_____

Names of participants   Roles

1 _____   _____

2 _____   _____

3 _____   _____

4 _____   _____

What did your group accomplish?

_____

_____

_____

What helped you get it done?

_____

_____

What got in your way? _____

_____

77

SUMMER
FUN

Not only are groups helpful when we're working, but when we're having fun as well. Below you will find a happy summer picture. Why is swimming an activity where groups are better?

Write a short paragraph giving your reasons on the lines below.

_____

_____

_____

_____

_____

_____

SECTION 8

Solving

Group

Problems

Pretend that you're working in your cooperative group. One of the group members, Becky, is very shy. Becky finds it hard to give her answers to the group and to tell others how she's feeling.

What can you do to help Becky become
more a part of the group?

What things might you say to Becky
to make her feel more at ease?

HOW WILL I ACT?

Picture yourself in your cooperative group. The newest member of the group is Reed who needs a wheelchair to help him get around. Reed is afraid the other group members will think he's "different."

How would you make Reed welcome in the group?

How would you treat him as a group member?

_____

_____

_____

_____

_____

PROBLEM TALK

Jenna is a member of your group. She thinks she does her work better alone and moves her chair away from the rest of the group to work.

**What will you say to Jenna
to help her become a good group member?**

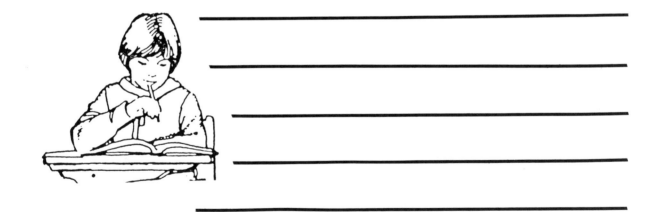

_____

_____

_____

_____

_____

_____

_____

NO PUT-DOWNS!

Sometimes during group discussions, Sam and Polly disagree and start calling each other names. They are forgetting a few important rules about working in groups. Can you help them remember these rules?

LISTENING HELP

Jeff likes to work in groups. He has a problem for you to help solve, though -- he would much rather talk than listen. Jeff enjoys talking so much that sometimes he forgets that others need a turn, too.

What suggestions would you give Jeff so he remembers to share discussion time with everyone?

Cooperative Repairs

All groups run into problems. With several of you working together closely, it will happen sooner or later. You will have a stronger group if you practice dealing with the problems as soon as they come up and solving them so you can get on with the task you are working together to accomplish. Think about your group. What can you remember about an assignment that didn't work out as well as it might have? On the lines below, describe it and what you think went wrong.

Curtain
Going Up . . .

On the following page you will find a short play about a group (like yours) which finds itself having problems. Your class and teacher can talk about how to use the play. Your group and each of the other groups could take the play and work on it together. Then the teacher could pick a group to perform it for the class.

The most important part is when you figure out what is making trouble for the group. Share your ideas with your group (or the whole class). Talk about possible solutions to use when your group is having that same problem or other problems like it.

The Case of the Unshared Computer

The characters are:

    Susan   Played by _____

    Jeff   Played by _____

    Paul   Played by _____

(The names of the characters are not important. If there are more girls in your group, choose girls' names instead -- or boys names if more are needed.)

As the scene opens, we see a group of three students working at their computer. They have a reading assignment which they are supposed to complete as a group.

JEFF: Susan, I think someone else should have a turn at the keyboard.

SUSAN: No! I can do it better than you and Paul can. I should be the one using the computer all the time.

PAUL: But if Jeff and I never get to try it, how can we get practice doing it?

SUSAN: That doesn't matter. We just want to get the assignment done as fast as possible and you and Jeff are too slow.

JEFF: But you thought that you should be the one who read the assignment, too.

SUSAN: That's because I'm a faster reader than you are.

JEFF: And you were the one who wrote down most of the answers to the questions.

SUSAN: Well, you're just too slow and it works better if I do it all.

Stop the Action! This Group has a Problem!

Solving the Case of the Unshared Computer

As you were acting out the scene on the preceding page, you began to notice that the group was having problems working cooperatively. What do you think caused some of those problems? List two things on the lines below.

_____

_____

_____

_____

What do you think would be possible solutions to the problems? How would you suggest that the group could work better together? List two suggestions on the lines below.

_____

_____

_____

_____

SECTION 9

Cooperating for a Friendly Class

Since you spend so much of your time at school, your classroom is really your "Home Away From Home." Picture what a warm, inviting, friendly place it would be if everyone worked and played there cooperatively!

Give a little thought to the areas listed below and suggest a few ways you think cooperation could be used.

IMPROVING THE WAY THE CLASSROOM LOOKS:

_____

_____

_____

_____

_____

HELPING YOUR TEACHER:

_____

_____

_____

_____

_____

_____

_____

SHOWING SUPPORT FOR YOUR CLASSMATES:

_____

_____

_____

_____

_____

_____

Cooperating
for a Friendly School

Keeping the school safe and comfortable and a place
you look forward to going to in the morning depends largely
upon the cooperation of each and every person who goes there.

Give your ideas about how people might work together
to solve the problems listed below.

KEEPING THE HALLWAYS AND LUNCHROOM PEACEFUL AND UNCLUTTERED.

_____

_____

_____

_____

STOPPING VANDALISM IN THE SCHOOL BATHROOMS

_____

_____

_____

ENDING GRAFFITI IN SCHOOL

_____

_____

_____

_____

_____

COOPERATIVE GHOSTS and GOBLINS

Halloween is a holiday where not only is it more <u>fun</u> to work cooperatively and do things in groups, but it is also more safe to do things together. Below you will find two groups of lines; see if you can think of ways in which Halloween would be safer and ways in which it would be more fun.

HALLOWEEN WOULD BE SAFER IF
WE DID THESE THINGS
IN GROUPS:

_____

_____

_____

_____

_____

HALLOWEEN WOULD BE MORE FUN
IF WE DID THESE THINGS
IN GROUPS:

_____

_____

_____

_____

_____

14   268IDA PB   4120
12/92 30910-124

© Johnson & Johnson